Are You With Me

New Women's Voices Series, No. 124

poems by

Lisa Katz

Finishing Line Press
Georgetown, Kentucky

Are You With Me

New Women's Voices Series, No. 124

Copyright © 2016 by Lisa Katz
ISBN 978-1-63534-020-4 First Edition
All rights reserved under International and Pan-American Copyright Conventions.
No part of this book may be reproduced in any manner whatsoever without written
permission from the publisher, except in the case of brief quotations embodied in critical
articles and reviews.

ACKNOWLEDGMENTS

Some of these poems appeared in *The Drunken Boat, Haaretz, Inkwell, The Jewish Quarterly of London, Leviathan Quarterly, Mississippi Review, Nimrod, Persimmon Tree, The Reading Room, Rhino* and *Illness in the Academy*, ed. Kimberly Myers, Purdue University Press, 2007. Some were published in Hebrew translation in *Shikhzur (Reconstruction)* Am Oved Press, Tel Aviv, 2008.

Publisher: Leah Maines

Editor: Christen Kincaid

Cover Art: Lisa Katz

Author Photo: Tineke de Lange

Cover Design: Elizabeth Maines

Printed in the USA on acid-free paper.
Order online: www.finishinglinepress.com
       also available on amazon.com

                     Author inquiries and mail orders:
                          Finishing Line Press
                            P. O. Box 1626
                      Georgetown, Kentucky 40324
                               U. S. A.

Table of Contents

Poem taped over my bed 1

Call to prayer 2

Not a pantoum 4

The secret of non-Euclidean geometry 5

B is for the birds 6

Are you with me 7

Leaning on the bar in Jerusalem with Walter Benjamin 8

Mattress moving 10

Reconstruction 14

The form 15

Chemotherapy 16

Post-op dream 17

Group 18

Breast art 19

My own Wikipedia 21

Heart 22

For Sylvia Plath 23

By Henry James 24

For Carmi and Maya

Poem taped over my bed

The poem I wrote when my dead mother shouted my name in a dream. *May no one steal your things,* she said, *in Barcelona.* The poem comprised of an ex-husband like a shrinking bear and one thousand nine hundred and forty nine boyfriends, in honor of the year of my birth. *May everyone treat you nicely.* A poem with breast-like funnels on a high ledge and one candle in a glass in a niche, a poem of meditation and yoga positions that exist only on this page. A poem that takes place in an old Middle Eastern city where I wait for shots to be fired, thrilled but not frightened. *You belong at home.* The poem that portrays my children sleeping every summer in a stucco building while a woman outside counts eggs. I hang my laundry on a line and in the poem it's stolen, my bras and bathing suits. *I told you so.* The poem appears in China on a poster of two pears cut in half, red inside and out. One-half pear is missing. The poem encompasses a large store wherein a boy calls out, "this neighborhood was happy once." *Love my daughter!* I want new bedding but we never arrive in that department. The poem claims that nakedness is also intelligence in my adopted language. In the tricky sense. Because of the snake. Never mind. Read only this, you who enter here, you know what we want.

Call to prayer

Don't call me, I can't come.
What once was a well
is dry as a wadi. I never
guessed it would be like this
my father said and I agree.
The wind is sere. Now me.

Gaza is arid and now me.
You called and I didn't come.
You say you disagree.
You're looking for an angel.
Samson was born of this.
And he asked God for water.

The meaning of forever
is eternal thirst for me.
Is that the prophecy?
Love called and I came,
water drawn from a well,
honey made by bees.

We're Philistines, don't you see.
Bondage is forever.
Delilah's no angel.
And the oasis is empty.
You call and I don't come.
Forever is like this.

I'm not promiscuous.
Not the bee and not the honey.
You call and I don't come.
Dew doesn't last forever.
You have the spirit, but not me.
I've plumbed the last of the well.

Religion dried the well.
I always expected this.
I didn't want to age, not me.
There is a hell, I agree,
for the non-believer.
You call and I can't come.

Agree or not, it's come to this.
That good well is gone forever.
The spirit wills, just not in me.

Not a pantoum

You stroked my left hand and held it.
I brushed your cheek with a palm.
The blinds fell from the window.
And my feet were over my head.
This is how friends make love.

This is how friends make love.
My feet were over my head.
The blinds fell from the window.
I brushed your cheek with a palm.
You stroked my left breast and cupped it.

I stroked your face resting on my shoulder.
My feet were over my head.
This is how friends make love.
The blinds fell from the window.

The blinds fell from the window.
This is how friends make love.
My feet were over my head.
My face brushed your cheek and I kissed you.

My feet pointed to the stars.
And the blinds fell around my head.

The secret of non-Euclidean geometry

I held the worn red book in my hands
its cover dulled by students
looking for answers

to the question assigned by the teacher
who sent us to the library
to learn about Euclid.

He wanted us to understand
Ibn al-Haytham and the Persians too.

Parallel lines meet somewhere in twisted space
in the curved world whose rules are false.

The flattened house
comes up behind me now,

a boy and a girl bear flowers away
to the place where all things converge

like the Mobius strip
which is never on the other side

of where we are.

B is for the birds

> *Israel is a bottleneck for migration routes;*
> *five hundred million pass through each year.*

Who came first?

The Indian silver bill established itself
along the Syrian-African rift in the 1920s.

The corncrakes and red-footed falcons
are just visiting, but

the bitterns are ours.
The northern wheatear has nothing to do

with wheat or ears.
A holdover from the Mandate,

like emergency regulations? Rare,
but a Kurdish wheatear was spotted in the Negev

during the war in Gaza. And Oriental skylarks
cross borders like foreign workers with wings.

Tree-tree-tree trill the little green bee-eaters,
not caring whose. Its multicolored sexes

look alike, which is against some beliefs.
O yellow wagtail and old world warblers,

fly catchers, sand grouse, shrikes and babblers,
sing *cuckoo*.

Are you with me

Let's say
you're inside me.
Are you with me?

Does the tent need the Bedouin?
Does the water need the camel?
Are you with me?

Let's say your leg rests on my leg.
Where are you going? Is it far?
Fingers in fingers,
you let out a cry.
The thread loves the needle
winding in and out.

Does the pillow need a sheet?
Your shoes, my feet.
The paper loves the pen
that inscribes.

Let's say you're staring
at the sky.
You want to be
Mount Everest itself.
Does the mountain need the Sherpa?
Are you with me?

Does the fire need the match?
The ring the finger?
The house its inhabitants?
The crown the tooth?
The umbrella loves the rain
pouring down.
Are you with me?

Leaning on the bar in Jerusalem with Walter Benjamin

During a time of terror
there is a desire
to overcome reality
by viewing its reproduction.

In my daughter's photograph
a woman sits with her back to us,
black hair falling downward
to the elastic rim of her strapless dress,
her right elbow leaning on the bar,
her hand holding sunglasses in motion
so that on film
they explode.
Two women lean toward her,
one with a closed and one with an open mouth.
Observation in a state of distraction
is increasing.

Three young women at the bar,
their bodies brim over their clothes
like foam. Identical ceramic teapots
imprinted with shooting stars
shoot their way across a shelf,
the room papered in stripes
whose flat ropes of thorny roses
ascend the wall. Outside
there is a separation wall but
the public
is absent-minded.

On the wooden bar, three
mobile phones, three packs of cigarettes,
two round plastic ashtrays
a cup filled with packets of sugar
and sugar substitutes,
a novelty ashtray topped by a ninja fighter,
and a collection box for orphaned children.
And to the right,
a tall beer siphon
topped with a handle
shaped like a grenade.
We experience our own destruction
as an aesthetic pleasure.

Mattress moving

1.

You could have walked up Broadway
and married a mannequin in the Gap window.
She would not slip her stiff hand
into your soul.
Store windows scare you.
So many choices.
All of them might be
wrong.
Uptown
there were women
awed by parachutes.
They washed and folded. And yet
you chose the one
who yawned, bought her
The Joy of Cooking
and a steam iron.

2.

The ring
on my infected finger
could not be removed with soap or butter.
The appropriate cutting tool was missing from our home.
The doctor in the emergency room
snapped it
in two.
I put the pieces in the change purse in my wallet
with a few small coins.
Our kitchen faced the street.
A thief entered our home
and stole the bag with the purse
with two halves of my ring.
The wire ring you bought for yourself
was too small.
You put in the drawer next to the bed,
the one you never opened
where you kept your dead father's ring,
too big.

3.

"Your writing was also your fear."
My writing was also your fear
a funhouse mirror
of our marriage
where you do not appear
until after dinner. O
the armchair of sacred rest.
Room for one. In the corridor
I danced the dance of seven veils
while you were dreaming
of your previous incarnation. Not the child
of refugee parents, mouths filled with words
ripped from the crazy quilt of Jewish Europe.
I studied the letters
of the backward-moving alphabet
that kidnapped you from the throne.
My voice
returned to the page.
You became an object
of interpretation.
I could live with mirror,
veil, chair and page,
metaphors filling
the space you left behind.

4.

You bought a big bed with a motor
and push button controls.   It rose and fell
at your command,
each mattress moving separately.
You tried it at the store,
bouncing on the sponge.
You were not a visitor
to my side. The bed cracked in two,
a long dry fissure down the middle
like Wadi Kelt in summer.
The line mocked me
at night
I could not cross it.
Even in dreams.

Reconstruction

You say I should rebuild
with a sack of plastic, or
one part of the body
replaces another.

A woman might love
a man without a leg.
They can have children.
And men whose legs
don't work
make children
with women who climb on.
Sometimes a child disappears
like a lost limb.

Couldn't we have
a different aesthetic,
asymmetrical,
Japanese,
because of the war,
because islands get invaded.

Couldn't we
admire the ruined, the torn, the perfect
error, because the weaver
skips a row
for the sake of humility,
because your love
needs a few stitches?

See the scar,
the flat plain on my chest.
Connect the dots.
You won't get many chances
to look at an absence straight on.

The form

Near Kastoria,
we were four kilometers from Metamorphosis
when I began to litter the road with my clothes,
and the foreign bra with one cup filled,
the new costume
of lopsided middle age.
You ask me
not to throw my human shape away.

Three kilometers from Metamorphosis.
When we get there I will accept
the transformation, for worse or better:
the wife into bird, the mother into stone.
Not least of all I want the story meaningful.

Two kilometers from Metamorphosis,
and though my nakedness suits me now,
it won't be easy
to wear the body I've chosen.

One more kilometer.

Chemotherapy

Someone new is crying.
She is going to lose her hair.
Dr. Olga sticks her with a needle,
and the nurses give her an infusion,
and the doctors hide in their rooms.
They say:
you will lose this organ
or that one.
We will make you sick.
You might get well again.

The social worker can arrange
money for some-
thing to stuff your bra,
free parking, and
a psychologist who will listen to you cry,
if you don't mind crying in front of strangers.

It was an arbitrary gene,
the electric station,
the wine, the stress, the mean
streak, my fault,
not my fault.

Post-op dream

I went into the basement to get a magazine.
I turned on the television and drank milk.
Two men came out of the storeroom
to drink milk and watch television.
We gaped at the girls on the television
in bikinis and tee shirts,
thousands of girls with two breasts each.
We drank until there was no more milk.
And the men whistled.
I had been a girl once too.
One put his hands on my waist.
The other touched me
and I said
I've only got one.
So they left.
I ran up the wooden stairs
two flights.
And locked the door.

Group

Five women are counting women
one by one, they want to count to five,
five cups, five eggs,
five oranges, five pearls,
five days a week to work.

Five women are counting women
one by one, they want to count to five.
And their children count the fingers on each hand:
father, mother, father, mother, father,
father, mother, father, mother, father.

There are so many new things to count.
The doctor who frowns *for your own good*
and the one who cuts
and the one who builds with plastic.
Time spent waiting.
For the first infusion
the second the third the fourth the fifth the last.
For hair to fall,
to grow back again,
for mirrors to grin
and spirits rise.

How time dies in the waiting room:
months weeks
days minutes
seconds.

Four women are counting women
One by one, they want to count to four.

Breast art

1.

Raphael`s *La Fornarina* lives in a Roman palace now,
touching her left breast, holding it between thumb and forefinger
like a fruit she wants to poke in the market.
Perhaps the artist asked her to demonstrate
beckoning a lover
plumping up the smaller breast
showing off in front of the mirror.
You think she's coy.
Perhaps she wanted to touch
the lump she noticed yesterday
as if she knows
the future will be here soon.

2.

In the church of the Frari in Venice
you look up at the ceiling.
You think you see the Virgin Mary
but it's just the artist's wife.
Her eyes roll upward.
She's transported with holiness
or her passion for Titian
and his for her,
but a gauze sash covers what's missing.
She'd rather look up than down.
The gaze is heavenward,
away from her flat earth.

3.

The Lady with the Ermine was a poet.
Leonardo painted her looking
as though she suddenly heard women crying
in the oncology ward,
women wearing helmets
attached to cooling machines
to keep their hair from falling out,
helmets like bonnets
anchored with a band around the forehead
and tied under the chin.
She froze listening.

The Lady with the Ermine wears beads
to add interest to the front of her dress.
They fall past the shadowy cavity.
She holds the furry animal to her flat chest,
close to the heart, which beats,
more loudly now, without the breast.

My own Wikipedia

Shelled walnuts look very much like the two halves of a brain. It is for this reason that the ancient Greeks and Romans believed that walnuts cured headaches. There was also a Roman belief that sleeping in the shade of a walnut tree caused headaches and uneasiness.

Think for me, walnut tree, think
as hard as your shells,
but no pain please.
You have so many hemispheres
to spare.
Protect me.
I sway in the wind
but your trunk stands
still, your upraised arms
cradle bird nests
near my fragile bed.
I hoard thoughts
but you don't want to hold on
to anything you own, dropping
the nuts one at a time,
each almost identical,
like a different version
of the same poem.
I close my mind
while you shed your leaves
that I sweep daily
in season. You give, I gather,
you stop, I wait
until you begin
to feed my uneasiness again.

Heart: corrections in The New York Times

A photograph of an anatomical drawing of a woman accompanying an article about an exhibition of Leonardo da Vinci's drawings at the Victoria and Albert Museum in London was provided by the museum in mirror image. The heart should have appeared on the right, not the left.

The review in the newspaper referred incorrectly to an early-17th-century Peruvian sculpture. The child Jesus in the sculpture holds half an avocado in his left hand, not half a heart.

Your heart was in the right place
but didn't weigh much because
suddenly you were born
after six months.
Send blood to the lungs
said the brain
but the heart refused
since changing plans
is humanly hard.
Send blood to the lungs
said the drugs which failed
because medicine
does not always work.
Send blood to the lungs
said the triumphant stitches.
Sometimes mechanical solutions
work best.
As for that avocado,
even Jesus would rather toy with his food
than his mother's heart.

For Sylvia Plath

Too many losses to count on the day that you died, everyone losing something at the same time: my friend Karen with a boy she never saw again, Frank with his girlfriend. And my childhood receding without a goodbye. But I didn't know you were drugged, unable to buy a stamp and mail your letter, your poems to the editor. But a pen is not enough when one dreams of perfection. I want to be complete myself. But does there have to be another person? And how close? I would never be Frank's first. On his birthday, I didn't know what was happening to any of you. It was only later I knew the whole story.

I was at the peak of my homemade ecstasy, or maybe I jolted in my dreams about a carnival, or I breathed quietly just as you were ending everything. Frank was coming for the first time not in a hand or a mouth. And afterward someone flushed a toilet. But by then you were gone.

By Henry James

But *if one marries at all*
one touches the earth, **the lady** *says.*

So she made herself small,
pretending there was less of her
than there really was.

He could tap
her imagination
with his knuckle
and make it ring. **But**
for him nothing in life
was a prize.

She had a certain way of looking
at life which he took as a personal offense. **But**
the sole source of her mistake
had been within herself.

Still *there were times*
when she thought
he enjoyed it. **So**
she saw the full moon —
she saw the whole man.

His egotism lay hidden
like a serpent in a bank of flowers.
It implied a sovereign contempt
for everyone but some three or four

very exalted people
whom he envied.

So *it was an opposition in which*
the vital principle of the one
was a thing of contempt to the other.

Still, she thought
the sole source of her mistake
had been within herself. **But**
wasn't all history full
of the destruction
of precious things?

If one marries at all.

Lisa Katz, (b. New York, in Israel since 1983), is editor of the Israeli pages of the Rotterdam-based *Poetry International Web*, http://www.poetryinternationalweb.net/pi/site/country/recent_list/12 and the author of *Shikhzur (Reconstruction)*, a book of her poems translated from English into Hebrew, (Am Oved Press, Tel Aviv, 2008).

An occasional book reviewer for the English edition of the daily *Haaretz* newspaper, she has translated books of selected works by Israeli poets Tuvia Ruebner (*Late Beauty* forthcoming from Zephyr in 2016), Admiel Kosman (*Approaching You in English Zephyr*, 2011) and Agi Mishol (Look There Graywolf, 2006).

Katz served as a lecturer in literary translation at Hebrew University, where she received her doctorate on the poetry of Sylvia Plath, https://www.academia.edu/11316748/What_Sylvia_Plath_Said_about_History_and_Womens_Lives and most recently at Ben Gurion University of the Negev. Her translation of "I have never needed God" by Israeli poet Miri Ben Simhon (1950-1996) appeared in *Poetry* in 2016.

www.ingramcontent.com/pod-product-compliance
Lightning Source LLC
LaVergne TN
LVHW052258070426
835507LV00036B/3386

9 781635 340204